Digital and Sustainable Trade Facilitation Implementation in the UNECE Region

UNECE Regional Report 2019

United Nations
Geneva, 2020

ECE/TRADE/448

ISBN: 978-92-1-117236-2
eISBN: 978-92-1-004770-8

FOREWORD

It is fair to say that trade facilitation is a key policy priority for most if not all the trading nations. The benefits for implementing trade facilitation provisions such as the ones in the World Trade Organization's (WTO) Trade Facilitation Agreement are well documented. However, the need for measuring progress of the provisions remain as strong as ever. Since 2015 the United Nations Global Survey on Digital and Sustainable Trade Facilitation has been successfully conducted by five United Nations Regional Commissions for Africa (ECA), Europe (ECE), Asia and the Pacific (ESCAP), Latin America and the Caribbean (ECLAC) and West Asia (ESCWA) with support from other UN agencies and international and regional organizations consecutively for the third time. For several years, this initiative has been a highlight of the Joint UNRC Approach to Trade Facilitation, agreed in Beirut in January 2010, by the Executive Secretaries of the five Regional Commissions.

In the UNECE region, the average implementation rate is higher than the global average reaching 72.6%, marking a 5.6%-percentage point increase since 2017. The survey for the region, covering a total of 42 member States shows improvement in all categories of measures. This year's survey includes a revamped-section on trade facilitation measures related to the 2030 Sustainable Development Agenda including SMEs, women participation and sectors like agriculture.

According to the survey, the measures included in the WTO Trade Facilitation Agreement have been generally well implemented by countries surveyed since their implementation in 2017. However, measures related to cross-border paperless trade implementation remains low compared other groups of measures, as do measures related to specific sectors and disadvantaged groups such as SMEs and women. Substantial effort is required to fully implement cross-border paperless, and to customize trade facilitation measures for SMEs and women.

This year, the survey results have been made available for further analysis in an online portal – www.untfsurvey.org.

Olga Algayerova
Executive Secretary
United Nations Economic Commission for Europe

Acknowledgement

The Third United Nations Global Survey on Digital and Sustainable Trade Facilitation 2019 has been jointly conducted by the five United Nations Regional Commissions. The United Nations Economic Commission for Europe (UNECE) led the survey for the Europe and Central Asia sub-regions. Under the overall guidance of Maria Ceccarelli, Officer-in-Charge, Economic Cooperation and Trade Division, the UNECE Regional Report for the Third United Nations Global Survey on Digital and Sustainable Trade Facilitation was prepared by Khan Salehin and Maria-Teresa Pisani. Data analysis support was provided by Charles Alexandre Frei.

Data collection was facilitated by the United Nations Centre for Trade Facilitation and Electronic Business (UN/CEFACT), an intergovernmental body serviced by UNECE; and the United Nations Network of Experts for Paperless Trade and Transport in Asia and the Pacific (UNNExT), a knowledge community supported by ESCAP and UNECE. Comments and suggestions received from participants at the UN Regional Commissions side event to the Global Review on Aid for Trade (Geneva, 4 July 2019), where the preliminary findings from the global survey were presented, are gratefully acknowledged.

The Report was edited by Karina van den Linden and publishing support was provided by Amélia Delle Foglie.

Contents

List of Figures

List of Tables

List of Boxes

Abbreviations

AEO	Authorized Economic Operator
ASEAN	Association of Southeast Asian Nations
ECA	United Nations Economic Commission for Africa
ESCAP	Economic and Social Commission for Asia and the Pacific
EU	European Union
ESCAP	Economic and Social Commission for Asia and the Pacific
ESCWA	Economic and Social Commission for the Western Asia
ICT	Information and Communication Technology
ITC	International Trade Centre
LDC	Least-Developed Country
LLDC	Landlocked Developing Country
NTFC	National Trade Facilitation Committee
OECD	Organization for Economic Cooperation and Development
SME	Small and Medium Enterprises
SPS	Sanitary and Phytosanitary
TFA	Trade Facilitation Agreement
UN/CEFACT	United Nations Centre for Trade Facilitation and Electronic Business
UNCTAD	United Nations Conference on Trade and Development
UNECE	United Nations Economic Commission for Europe
UNRC	United Nations Regional Commission
WTO	World Trade Organization
WTO TFA	World Trade Organization Trade Facilitation Agreement

1. Introduction

1.1 Background and objective of the Global Survey on Digital and Sustainable Trade Facilitation 2019

Facilitating trade and reducing trade barriers is of central importance to the economies of the United Nations Economic Commission for Europe (UNECE) as it enables them to better connect and gain from regional and global value chains and to fully harness the potential of trade as an engine for growth and sustainable development. Yet, both in the UNECE region and globally, trade barriers remain high. According to the latest data from the ESCAP-World Bank International Trade Cost Database, the overall cost of trading goods among the three largest European Union (EU) economies remains at a 42% average tariff on the valué of traded goods (see Table 1) while it reaches a peak of 169% for trading with South-Eastern Europe. Similarly, the cost of trading among Central Asian countries averages 75%, while it reaches 153% with the three largest EU countries. This shows that there is still much to be done to cut the "red-tape" that exists in moving goods across borders and that this poses a particular burden on small and medium sized-enterprises in both developed and emerging economies. This report provides an overview of the progress made in sustainable and digital trade facilitation within countries of the UNECE region. It identifies the areas where the most progress has been made, and also those areas where implementation challenges remain. The goal is to help focus the efforts of the UNECE governments and international cooperation programs in those areas where policy, legal, regulatory and technical gaps exist.

Table 1: Intra- and extra-regional comprehensive trade costs (excluding tariff costs)

	Caucasus and Turkey	Central Asia	Eastern Europe	EU-3	SE Europe	Canada
Caucasus and Turkey	174.0% (5.4%)	182.1% (1.0%)	145.9% (-3.1%)	153.1% (-0.9%)	322.9% (-12.0%)	185.5% (-7.6%)
Central Asia	182.1% (1.0%)	75.4% (4.4%)	150.1% (5.2%)	177.4% (-3.4%)	346.2% (-2.7%)	220.8% (1.4%)
Eastern Europe	145.9% (-3.1%)	150.1% (5.2%)	70.2% (-4.0%)	122.4% (-7.9%)	272.2% (-17.4%)	239.9% (-7.8%)
EU-3	153.1% (-0.9%)	177.4% (-3.4%)	122.4% (-7.9%)	42.1% (-5.6%)	168.6% (-10.6%)	85.5% (-4.1%)
South-Eastern Europe	322.9% (-12.0%)	346.2% (-2.7%)	272.2% (-17.4%)	168.6% (-10.6%)	91.3% (-14.1%)	268.7% (-6.3%)
Canada	185.5% (-7.6%)	220.8% (1.4%)	239.9% (-7.8%)	85.5% (-4.1%)	268.7% (-6.3%)	
Russian Federation	97.0% (-7.9%)	80.3% (3.6%)	68.8% (-12.5%)	79.7% (1.9%)	200.1% (-9.2%)	145.1% (-4.0%)

Source: ESCAP-World Bank Trade Cost Database, updated June 2019. Available from https://artnet.unescap.org/databases#tradecost and https://www.unescap.org/resources/escap-world-bank-trade-cost-database.

Notes: Trade costs may be interpreted as tariff equivalents. Percentage changes in trade costs between 2006-2011 and 2012-2017 are in parentheses.

Caucasus and Turkey: Armenia, Azerbaijan, Georgia, Turkey; **Central Asia**: Kazakhstan, Kyrgyzstan; **Eastern Europe**: Belarus, Moldova, Ukraine; **EU-3**: Germany, France, United Kingdom; **South-Eastern Europe**: Albania, Macedonia, Montenegro.

In the UNECE region, trade cost reduction has been mostly achieved though the elimination or lowering of tariffs. Going forward, further trade cost reductions could be obtained by addressing non-tariff sources of trade barriers such as sanitary or phytosanitary measures, inefficient transport and logistics infrastructure and services, and hefty and inefficient regulatory procedures and documentary requirements.

Recent international and regional initiatives (such as the WTO TFA and the Framework Agreement on Facilitation of Cross-border Paperless Trade in Asia and the Pacific) have introduced a wide range of measures for expediting the movement, release and clearance of goods (including goods in transit); for effective cooperation between customs and other appropriate authorities on trade facilitation and customs compliance issues; and for digital and paperless trade. At the same time, under the Joint Approach to Trade Facilitation of the United Nations Regional Commissions (UNRCs), and following extensive discussions at the Global Trade Facilitation Forum in 2013, it was decided that regional surveys should be conducted by all UNRCs. Since then, the UNRCs have been systematically collecting and analysing data and information on the implementation of measures for trade facilitation and paperless trade and two global and regional surveys were conducted in 2015 and 2017. This report is a continuation of these efforts and features the results of a third regional survey (conducted in 2019) involving 42 economies from 7 subregions of the UNECE region.

Following an introduction to the survey instrument and methodology, a region-wide overview of the implementation of trade facilitation measures across countries and subregions is provided in Section 2. This is followed by a closer look at the implementation levels of various groups of trade facilitation measures in Section 3. Finally, the report highlights key findings and proposes a way forward for advancing sustainable and digital trade facilitation in Section 4.

1.2   2019 Survey instrument and methodology

The United Nations Global and Regional Survey on Digital and Sustainable Trade Facilitation 2019 covers the full list of provisions included in the World Trade Organization Trade Facilitation Agreement (WTO TFA) and the regional United Nations treaty: the Framework Agreement on Facilitation of Cross-Border Paperless Trade in Asia and the Pacific.

The Survey, conducted by the five UNRCs, comprises 50 detailed common trade facilitation measures, categorized into three groups and nine subgroups. The first group, General Trade Facilitation Measures, includes WTO TFA measures under four subgroups: Transparency; Formalities; Institutional Cooperation and Arrangement; and Transit Facilitation. The second group, Digital Trade Facilitation Measures, includes two subgroups: Paperless Trade and Cross-Border Paperless Trade. The third group, Sustainable Trade Facilitation Measures, includes three subgroups: Trade Facilitation for SMEs; Agricultural Trade Facilitation; and Women in Trade Facilitation. In 2019, some Regional Commissions introduced a fourth group, called Trade Finance Facilitation Measures, as a pilot project. This was developed in cooperation with the International Chamber of Commerce (ICC) Banking Commission.

The overall scope of the survey goes beyond the measures included in the WTO TFA. Most paperless trade and cross-border paperless trade measures are not specifically featured in the WTO TFA, although their implementation (in many cases) would support better implementation of the WTO TFA measures in digital form. Most of the surveyed measures included in the Sustainable Trade Facilitation group are also not specifically included in the WTO TFA, except for some of the Agricultural Trade Facilitation measures (see Table 2).

Table 2: Grouping of trade facilitation measures and their correspondence with TFA articles

Grouping		Question #		Trade facilitation measure in the questionnaire	TFA Articles
		2017	2019		
General TF measures	Transparency (5 measures)	2	2	Publication of existing import-export regulations on the Internet	1.2
		3	3	Stakeholder consultation on new draft regulations (prior to their finalization)	2.2
		4	4	Advance publication/notification of new regulations before their implementation (e.g. 30 days prior)	2.1
		5	5	Advance ruling (on tariff classification)	3
		9	9	Independent appeal mechanism (for traders to appeal customs rulings and the rulings of other relevant trade control agencies)	4
	Formalities (8 measures)	6	6	Risk management (as a basis for deciding whether a shipment will be physically inspected or not)	7.4
		7	7	Pre-arrival processing	7.1
		8	8	Post-clearance audit	7.5
		10	10	Separation of Release from final determination of customs duties, taxes, fees and charges	7.3
		11	11	Establishment and publication of average release times	7.6
		12	12	Trade facilitation measures for authorized operators	7.7
		13	13	Expedited shipments	7.8
		14	14	Acceptance of paper or electronic copies of supporting documents required for import, export or transit formalities	10.2.1
	Institutional cooperation and arrangement (5 measures)	1	1	Establishment of a national trade facilitation committee or similar body	23
		31	31	Cooperation between agencies on the ground at the national level	8
		32	32	Government agencies delegating controls to customs authorities	
		33	33	Alignment of working days and hours with neighbouring countries at border crossings	8.2(a)
		34	34	Alignment of formalities and procedures with neighbouring countries at border crossings	8.2(b)
Digit	Paperless trade (10 measures)	15	15	Electronic/automated Customs System established (e.g. ASYCUDA)	

Grouping		Question #		Trade facilitation measure in the questionnaire	TFA Articles
		2017	2019		
		16	16	Internet connection available to customs and other trade control agencies at border crossings	
		17	17	Electronic Single Window system	10.4
		18	18	Electronic submission of customs declarations	
		19	19	Electronic application and issuance of Import and Export Permit	
		20	20	Electronic submission of sea cargo manifests	
		21	21	Electronic submission of air cargo manifests	
		22	22	Electronic application and issuance of Preferential Certificate of Origin	
		23	23	E-Payment of customs duties and fees	7.2
		24	24	Electronic application for customs refunds	
	Cross-border paperless trade (6 measures)	25	25	Laws and regulations for electronic transactions are in place (e.g. e-commerce law, e-transaction law)	
		26	26	Recognized certification authority issuing digital certificates to traders to conduct electronic transactions	
		27	27	Customs declaration electronically exchanged between your country and other countries	
		28	28	Certificate of Origin electronically exchanged between your country and other countries	
		29	29	Sanitary & Phytosanitary Certificate electronically exchanged between your country and other countries	
		30	30	Banks and insurers in your country retrieving letters of credit electronically without lodging paper-based documents	
Sustainable TF Measures	Transit facilitation (4 measures)	35	35	Transit facilitation agreement(s) with neighbouring country(ies)	
		36	36	Customs Authorities limit the physical inspection of transit goods and use risk assessment	10.5
		37	37	Supporting pre-arrival processing for transit facilitation	11.9
		38	38	Cooperation between agencies of countries involved in transit	11.16
	Trade facilitation for SMEs (5 measures)	39	39	Government has developed trade facilitation measures that ensure easy and affordable access for SMEs to trade-related information	
		40	40	Government has developed specific measures that enable SMEs to more easily benefit from the AEO scheme	
		41	41	Government has taken actions to make single windows more easily accessible to SMEs (e.g. by providing technical consultation and training services to SMEs on registering and using the facility.)	
		42	42	Government has taken actions to ensure that SMEs are well represented and made key members of National Trade Facilitation Committees (NTFCs)	
			43	Implementation of other special measures to reduce costs for SMEs	

Grouping		Question #		Trade facilitation measure in the	TFA Articles
		2017	2019	questionnaire	
	Agricultural trade facilitation (4 measures)	43	44	Testing and laboratory facilities are equipped for compliance with sanitary and phytosanitary (SPS) standards in your main trading partners	
		44	45	National standards and accreditation bodies are established for the purpose of compliance with SPS standards	
		45	46	Application, verification and issuance of SPS certificates is automated	
			47	Special treatment given to perishable goods at border-crossings	7.9
	Women in trade facilitation (3 measures)	46	48	The existing trade facilitation policy/strategy incorporates special consideration of women involved in trade	
		47	49	Government has introduced trade facilitation measures aimed at women involved in trade	
			50	Female membership in the National Trade Facilitation Committee	
Trade finance facilitation (3 measures)			51	Single Window facilitates traders with access to finance	
			52	Banks allow electronic exchange of data between trading partners or with banks in other countries to reduce dependence on paper documentation and advance digital trade	
			53	A variety of trade finance services available	

Source: The Second UNRC Survey on Trade Facilitation and Paperless Trade and the Third United Nations Survey on Digital and Sustainable Trade Facilitation

For data collection and validation the UNRCs adopted a three-step approach (see Table 3) consisting of (1) gathering preliminary information from experts and committees; (2) data verification through a combination of desk research, phone interviews and sharing with other key regional and international partner organizations in trade facilitation; and (3) submission of the data set to UNECE member states for their final review and confirmation.

Table 3: The three-step approach for data collection and validation

Step 1. Data submission by experts: The survey instrument was sent by the UNECE Secretariat to trade facilitation experts and committees (governments, permanent missions, the private sector and academia) in UNECE countries to gather preliminary information. The questionnaire was also made publicly available online and disseminated with the support of the United Nations Centre for Trade Facilitation and Electronic Business (UN/CEFACT), OECD, ITC, and UNCTAD. In some cases, the questionnaire was also sent to relevant national trade facilitation authorities or agencies and regional trade facilitation partners or organizations. This first step took place roughly between January and April 2019.

Step 2. Data verification by the UNECE Secretariat: The UNECE Secretariat double checked the data collected in Step 1. Desk research and data sharing among regional commissions of the United Nations and survey partners were carried out to further check the accuracy of data. Face-to-face or telephone interviews with key informants were arranged to gather additional information when needed. The outcome of Step 2 was a consistent set of responses per country. Step 2 took place between January and April 2019.

Step 3. Data validation by national governments: The UNECE Secretariat sent the completed questionnaire to each national government to ensure that the country had the opportunity to review the data set and provide any additional information. This feedback from national governments was incorporated in order to finalize the data set. Step 3 took place between April and June 2019.

Based on the data collected, each of the trade facilitation measures included in the Survey was rated as "fully implemented", "partially implemented", "on a pilot basis", or "not implemented". Definitions for each stage are provided below. A score (weight) of 3, 2, 1 or 0 was assigned to each of the four implementation stages to calculate implementation scores for individual measures across countries, regions or categories. Country groupings used in the analysis were defined by UNECE in 2017 (see Table 4).

Table 4: Definition of each stage of implementation

- **Full Implementation**: The trade facilitation measure is implemented in full compliance with commonly-accepted international standards, recommendations and conventions such as the Revised Kyoto Convention, UN/CEFACT Recommendations, or the WTO TFA; it is implemented in law and in practice; it is available to all relevant stakeholders nationwide and is supported by adequate legal and institutional frameworks as well as adequate infrastructure and financial and human resources. A TFA provision included in the commitments given under Notifications of Category A may generally be considered as a measure which is fully implemented by the country, with a caveat that the provision will be implemented by a Least-Developed Country (LDC) member within one year of the TFA agreement coming into force. If a country registers positive responses for all sub-questions concerning a given trade facilitation measure, that measure should be considered fully implemented.

- **Partial Implementation**: A measure is considered to be partially implemented if at least one of the following is true: (1) the trade facilitation measure is in partial - but not in full - compliance with commonly-accepted international standards, recommendations and conventions; (2) the country is still in the process of rolling out the implementation of the measure; (3) the measure is being used but on an unsustainable, short-term or ad-hoc basis; (4) the measure is implemented in some - but not all - targeted locations (such as key border-crossing stations); or (5) some - but not all - targeted stakeholders are fully involved.

- **Pilot Stage of Implementation**: A measure is considered to be in the pilot stage of implementation if, in addition to meeting the general attributes of partial implementation, it is available only to a very small portion of the intended stakeholder group (or at certain location) and/or is being implemented on a trial basis. When a new trade facilitation measure is at the pilot stage of implementation, the old measure is often used in parallel to ensure that service can continue in the case of disruptions associated with the new measure. This stage of implementation also includes relevant rehearsals and preparation for the full implementation.

- **Not implemented**: A measure has not been implemented at this stage. However, this stage may include initiatives or efforts made toward implementation of the measure. For example, under this stage, (pre)feasibility studies or planning for the implementation can be carried out and consultation with stakeholders on the implementation may be arranged.

2. Trade facilitation implementation in Europe, Central Asia and North America: Overview

The average implementation rate of trade facilitation has reached 72.6% in Europe, Central Asia and North America. This marks a sensible improvement, compared to the average implementation of 67%[1] showed in the Survey conducted in 2017. All the subregions within UNECE have contributed positively to this improvement (see Figure 1). Advanced countries are leading in terms of average trade facilitation implementation, and among the 42 countries that participated in the Survey, the Netherlands and Belgium jointly top the list of best performers with about 94% implementation. The non-developed economies show varying levels of implementation, with some reaching the same levels of developed economies and others performing much below the UNECE average rate. Among the non-developed or transition economies, the Republic of North Macedonia and Azerbaijan are at the top, with about 82% implementation. Turkey and Georgia also performed very well, with implementation around 80%, while in the Eastern European subregion, Belarus stands out with 72% implementation. On the other hand, emerging economies who achieved lower implementation include Bosnia and Herzegovina (41%) and Albania (53%).

Figure 1: Trade facilitation implementation in the UNECE region, 2019

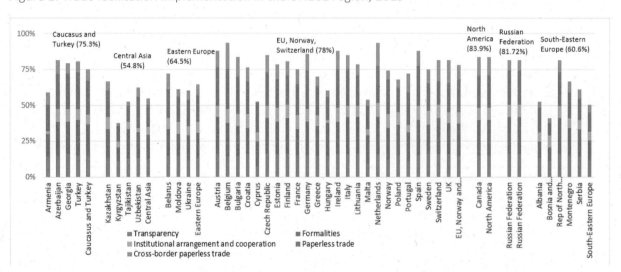

Overall, more advanced economies in the region are doing better than smaller or less advanced economies in facilitating their trade procedures and are achieving higher implementation rates. Figure 2 highlights a positive correlation between trade facilitation implementation and GDP per capita for UNECE member states, which confirms the trend of the 2017 Survey.

---

[1] The average implementation was about 69% in 2017. However, some scoring adjustments were made based on 2019 data.

Figure 2: Trade Facilitation implementation and GDP per capita in the UNECE region

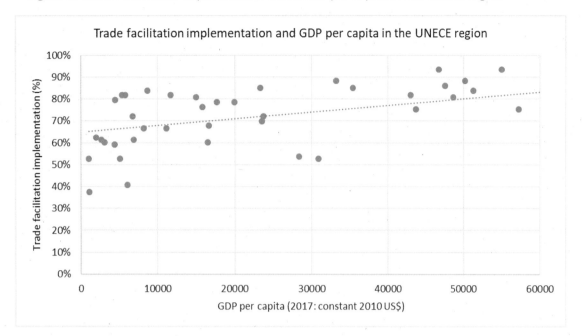

2.1   Implementation in the subregions

Figure 3 provides an overview of implementation rates in the various UNECE subregions. The North American; Russian Federation and EU; and Norway and Switzerland subregions reached 84%, 80.6%, and 78% implementation respectively. EU countries have had moderate to high implementation rates with the exception of two member states that reached 50%. The EU group is followed by Caucasus and Turkey, the Russian Federation and the Eastern Europe subregions with an average implementation between 65% and 73%. South-Eastern Europe exceeded 60% implementation, thanks to the strong performance of two countries in the subregion. Central Asia have the lowest average implementation rate in the region reaching approximately 55%.

Figure 3: Trade facilitation implementation in subregions

- The coloured circles represent the trade facilitation implementation of individual countries in respective subregions (in percentage).
— The coloured line represents the average implementation level by respective subregions

The implementation rates within the subregions vary significantly, with the greatest variation in the South-Eastern European countries. This group includes both one of the highest-performing countries and one of the lowest-performing countries of the UNECE region. Differences among the countries also exist in the EU, Norway and Switzerland subregion. The Central Asian subregion also includes a varying-level of implementation among its countries.

The UNECE region includes several landlocked developing economies, for which the Implementation of trade facilitation measures is particularly challenging due to the landlocked nature of their territory. However, as shown in figure 3, some countries are more advanced than others—once again showing a difference of implementation rates.

Figure 4: Trade facilitation implementation by categories in the UNECE region

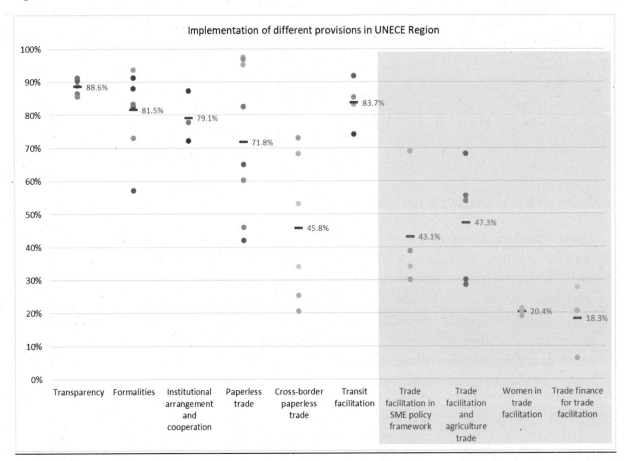

- Coloured circles show average implementation-levels of individual measures in each category
- Coloured lines show the average regional implementation-levels for each category

The trade facilitation measures surveyed in this report, are grouped into multiple categories. Figure 4 shows that all the countries of the UNECE region are well advanced in the implementation of general trade facilitation measures including transparency, formalities and institutional arrangement and cooperation categories. The transparency category was implemented the most with an average implementation of 88.6%. Formalities and Institutional Arrangement . and Cooperation were implemented on average at 81.5% and 79.1% respectively. Paperless trade was relatively less implemented with an average implementation of 71.8%. Cross-border paperless trade was the least-implemented category of measures with an average implementation of 45.8%. Transit facilitation was pursued very strongly, as evident with an average of 83.7% implementation.

The implementation of sustainable trade facilitation measures, including, for instance, the facilitation of cross-border exchanges for SMEs or women involved in trade or agricultural perishable goods, is slowly receiving prominence in the trade facilitation agenda—although they have not reached the levels of the general trade facilitation measures. As figure 4 shows, agriculture trade-related measures and trade facilitation in SME policy framework have an average implementation of 47.3% and 43.1% respectively, indicating low implementation in general. Furthermore, very few countries implemented measures related to participation of women in trade and trade finance for trade facilitation as reflected in the lowest average implementation among all the categories at 20.4% and 18.3% respectively.

2.2 Most and least implemented trade facilitation measures

Table 5 provides a list of the most and least-implemented measures under each category. In the transparency and formality categories, for example, stakeholder consultation on new draft regulations and risk management have been implemented fully, partially or on a pilot-basis by all the countries. In the paperless trade category, automated customs systems have also been implemented by all countries. In cross-border paperless trade, laws and regulations for electronic transactions have been implemented by 90% of the countries, which demonstrates that the countries are developing their legal frameworks for digitalization for cross-border trade.

Table 5: Most and least-implemented measures across the categories in the UNECE region

Category	Most implemented (% of countries)		Least implemented (% of countries)	
	Measure	Implemented fully, partially and on a pilot basis/Full implementation (%)	Measure	Implemented fully, partially and on a pilot basis/Full implementation (%)
Transparency	Stakeholders' consultation on new draft regulations (prior to their finalization)	100/69	Advance publication/notification of new trade-related regulations before their implementation	95.2/73.8
Formalities	Risk Management	100/81	Separation of Release from final determination of customs duties, taxes, fees and charges	71.4/34.8
Institutional arrangement and cooperation	National legislative framework and/or institutional arrangements for border agencies cooperation	100/64.3	National Trade Facilitation Committee or similar body	83.3/76.1
Paperless trade	Automated Customs System	100/92.9	Electronic application and issuance of	54.8/23.8

			Preferential Certificate of Origin	
Cross-border paperless trade	Laws and regulations for electronic transactions	90.5/35.7	Electronic exchange of Certificate of Origin	33.3/4.8
Transit facilitation	Customs Authorities limit the physical inspections of transit goods and use risk assessment	92.9/83.3	Transit facilitation agreement(s)	78.6/59.5
Trade facilitation in SME policy framework	Trade facilitation measures targeting SMEs	78.6/52.4	Ease compliance of SMEs to trade procedures	40.5/9.5
Trade facilitation and agriculture trade	Testing and laboratory facilities available to meet SPS of main trading partners	73.8/47.6	Electronic application and issuance of SPS certificates	45.2/7.1
Women in trade facilitation	Trade facilitation measures to benefit female traders	33.3/0.0	Trade facilitation policy/strategy incorporates special consideration for female traders	28.6/9.5
Trade finance for trade facilitation	Trade finance services available	35.7/16.7	Single window facilitates traders in access to finance	7.1/4.8

Source: United Nations Global Survey on Digital and Sustainable Trade Facilitation, 2019.

2.3 Progress in implementation between 2017 and 2019

The average implementation of the 31 trade facilitation measures in the survey increased by five percentage points[2] between 2017 and 2019 rising to 72.6%. This average includes results from the six new countries that participated in the 2019 Survey. The 2019 average implementation without these countries stood at 73.5%. The Caucasus and Turkey subregion improved its performance by 13 percentage points and reached 75%. The Central Asian subregion increased implementation from 39% to about 55%, which is the highest improvement in the UNECE region, although the baseline was low in 2017. The Eastern European subregion saw a rise from 58% to 64% while South-Eastern Europe

---

[2] The average implementation was about 69% in 2017. However, some scoring adjustments were made based on 2019 data and the revised average implementation stands at about 67%.

improved implementation from 56% to about 61%. The EU, Norway and Switzerland region also progressed slightly from an already strong 76% in 2017 to 78% in 2019.

Figure 5: Trade Facilitation Implementation in the subregions – 2017 and 2019

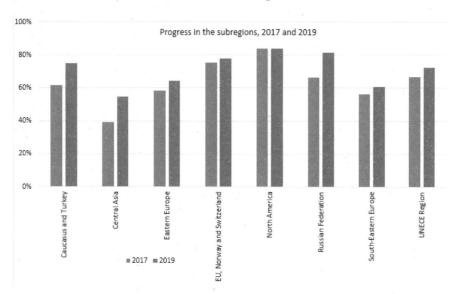

Figure 6: Evolution of the trade facilitation categories – 2017 and 2019

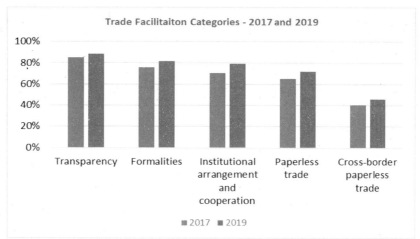

All the trade facilitation categories of measures have higher average implementation in 2019 than in 2017. The greatest improvement was made in institutional arrangement and cooperation, which rose from 71% in 2017 to 79% in 2019. Implementation of transparency and formalities measures reached 88% from 85%, and 81% from 76% respectively. For digital measures too, the average implementation improved—for paperless trade and cross-border paperless trade in particular. These rose from 65% to 71% and 41% to 46% respectively.

Figure 7 shows the improvements of the subregions in every category between 2017 and 2019. As the figures suggests, Caucasus and Turkey improved the most in transparency while performance in South-Eastern Europe deteriorated slightly[3]. The Russian Federation, and Caucasus and Turkey subgroups made significant progress in formalities. In institutional arrangement and cooperation, the Caucasus and Turkey and Central Asia regions made the most progress. In paperless trade, the Russian

_____

[3] In the 2019 survey, South-Eastern Europe included one new country with very low implementation and hence the average implementation of the subregion was impacted.

Federation and Central Asia advanced most while in cross-border paperless trade, Central Asia's improvement is significant.

Figure 7: Improvements in the subregions – 2017 and 2019

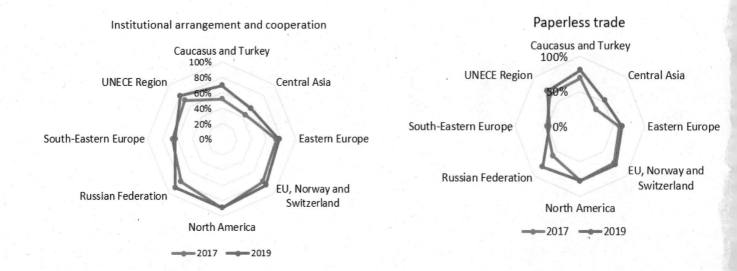

Top Reformer between 2017 and 2019 in the UNECE Region: Kazakhstan

Kazakhstan is one of the top reformers of trade facilitation in the UNECE region since the last Survey in 2017. According to the 2019 survey, the country's implementation reached 66.7% which is 20 percentage points more than the 2017 survey. The rapid improvement is due to strong performance in general as well as in digital trade facilitation measures. In early 2018, Kazakhstan fully established their National Trade Facilitation Committee and since then it has been functioning as a platform for policy discussions among government agencies and private sector representatives, including the National Chamber of Entrepreneurs. Strong efforts have been devoted to the establishment of a Single Window system. It has been pilot-tested and the formal launch is expected to take place by the end of 2019. On the digital front, Kazakhstan's advancement is noteworthy. For example, since January 2018, all customs declarations have been carried out electronically. Moreover, it has fully operationalized the electronic payment systems of customs duties and fees. The information on payments is received online through the payment gateway of the Government, eGOV.kz. Almost all banks (26 out of 29) have been connected to the gateway. Although on a pilot basis, since May 2018, preferential certificates of origin can be applied for and obtained electronically. The certificates are processed and issued by designated organizations in accordance with international agreements. In addition, significant progress has been made in the electronic exchange of customs declarations with other countries, including those of the Eurasian Economic Union, and Uzbekistan.

Source: United Nations Global Survey on Digital and Sustainable Trade Facilitation 2019

Cross-border paperless trade

Box 1: Top reformer in the UNECE region since 2017

3. Implementation of trade facilitation measures: a closer Look

This chapter will take an in-depth look inside the results of the UNECE 2019 survey by analysing measure-by-measure the scores of the UNECE region and its country groups or subregions. The survey has separated the questionnaire into eleven different sub-categories, regrouping several questions as indicators of implementation of a certain measure. Eleven different measures have been identified such as transparency, formalities, institutional arrangement and cooperation, paperless trade, cross-border paperless trade, transit facilitation, trade facilitation for SMEs, agricultural trade facilitation, women in trade facilitation and trade finance for trade facilitation measures.

3.1 "Transparency" Measures

Five trade facilitation measures included in the Survey are categorized as "transparency" measures. They relate to Articles 1-5 of the WTO TFA and GATT[4] Article X on publication and administration of trade regulations. The average level of implementation for all five "transparency" measures across the entire region reached 88.57%, with North America followed by the European Union, Norway and Switzerland achieving almost full implementation. Indeed, Canada reached a full score in the implementation of the *independent appeal mechanism*, *advance ruling on tariff classification and origin of imported goods*, and *advance publication/notification of new trade-related regulations*. *Advance ruling on tariff classification and origin of imported goods* is the least implemented measure in this category, with the lowest implementation levels occurring in Central Asia and South-Eastern Europe.

Figure 8: Implementation of "transparency" measures: UNECE average, 2019

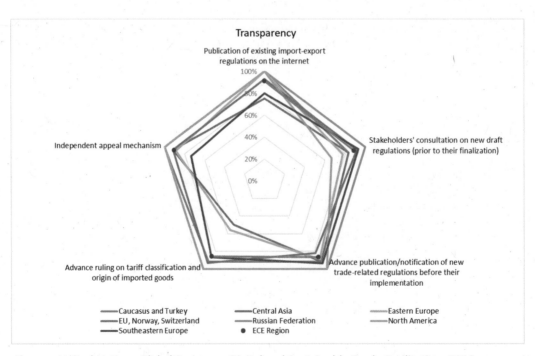

Source: United Nations Global Survey on Digital and Sustainable Trade Facilitation, 2019

---

[4] General Agreement on Tariffs and Trade (1994). Available at:
https://www.wto.org/english/docs_e/legal_e/gatt47_01_e.htm#articleX

Figure 9 ranks all countries of the UNECE region by measures that are either fully and partially-implemented; at a pilot stage; or not implemented. Measures are ranked in descending order. *Stakeholder consultation on new draft regulations* (*prior to their finalization*), *publication of existing import-export regulations on the internet,* and *independent appeal mechanism* are the most implemented "transparency" measures in the region as over 95% of the 42 countries surveyed fully or partially implemented them.

Figure 9: Implementation of "transparency" measures for trade facilitation in UNECE economies, 2019

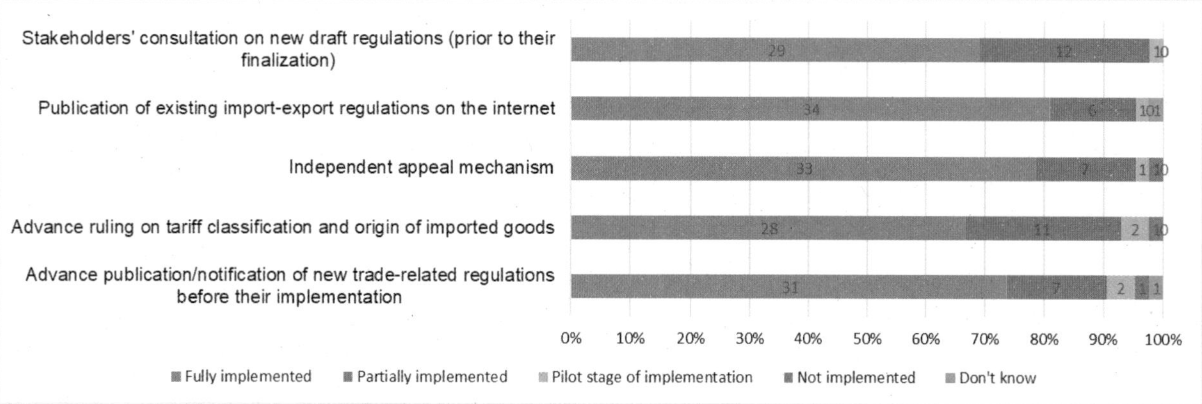

Source: United Nations Global Survey on Digital and Sustainable Trade Facilitation, 2019

Advance ruling (on tariff classification) and advance publication/notification of new trade-related regulations before their implementation have been relatively less implemented. However, the former has been already either fully or partially implemented by 92.9% of countries (or 39 countries) in the region and the latter by 90.5% of countries (or 38 countries). For both measures, only one country has not implemented them yet.

3.2   "Formalities" measures

The eight surveyed "formalities" measures are related to Articles 6-10 of the WTO TFA, and GATT Article VIII on Fees and Formalities connected with Importation and Exportation. While the average implementation of this category of measures is 81.5%, figure 10 shows a contrast in terms of the level of implementation for the measures. *Risk management*; *acceptance of copies of original supporting documents required for import-export*; *post-clearance audits*; and *Separation of Release from final determination of customs duties, taxes, fees and charges* have been relatively well implemented in the region. However, *pre-arrival processing*; *establishment and publication of average release times*; *expedited shipments*; and *trade facilitation measures for authorized operators* have been implemented at varying levels, including in Central Asia which has lowest average implementation. Eastern European countries implemented these measures at a lower rate, except *trade facilitation measures for authorized operators*, which they implemented fully. South-Eastern Europe has room for improvement in these measures too.

Figure 10: Implementation of trade "formalities" facilitation measures: UNECE average, 2019

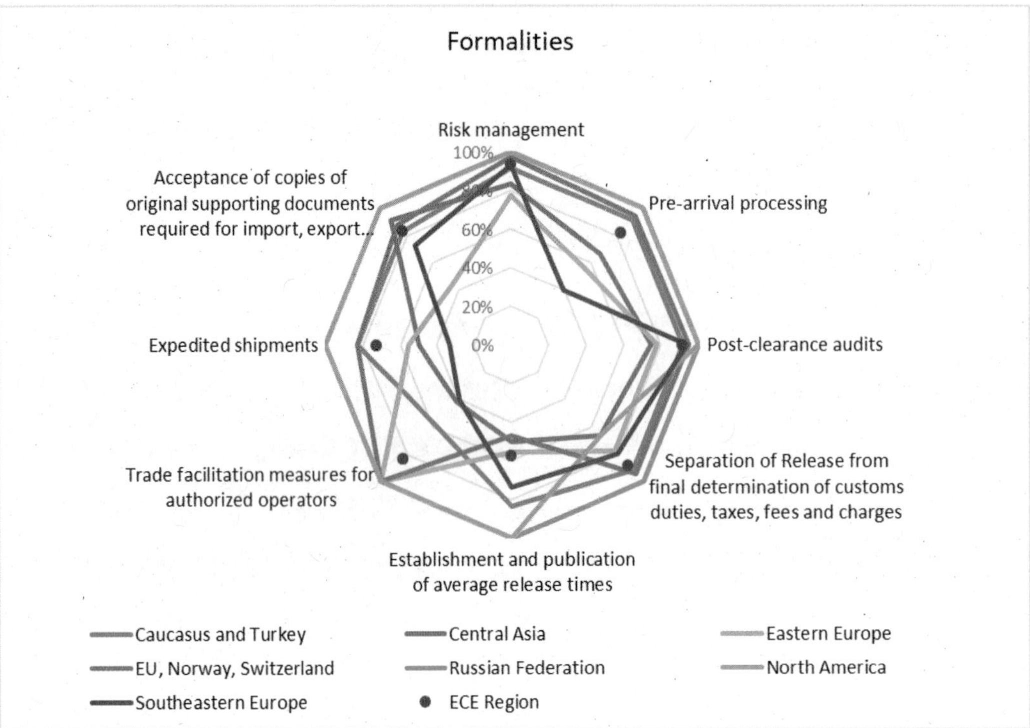

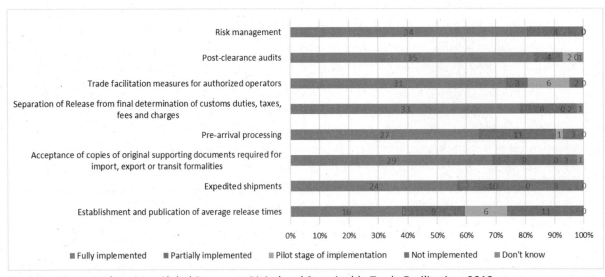

Source: United Nations Global Survey on Digital and Sustainable Trade Facilitation, 2019

Figure 11 shows the status of each measure according to the number of countries that implemented them. *Risk management* has been implemented by all the countries in the region either fully or partially. *Post-clearance audit* and *Separation of Release from final determination of customs duties, taxes, fees and charges* have been implemented by 92.8% of them (39 countries). On the contrary, *establishment and publication of average release times* has been fully implemented by only 38% of countries (16 countries) and 59.5% of countries (25 countries) if partial implemented is counted.

Figure 11: Implementation of trade "formalities" facilitation measures in UNECE economies, 2019

Source: United Nations Global Survey on Digital and Sustainable Trade Facilitation, 2019

3.3   "Institutional arrangement and cooperation" measures

Figure 12 shows the average implementation levels of the "Institutional arrangement and cooperation" measures. The average implementation of this category of measures is 79.1% in the UNECE region. *National legislative framework and institutional arrangement for border agencies cooperation* has been highly implemented by most of the subregions. The *national trade facilitation committee* has also been implemented, although to a slightly lesser extent in some subregions. In contrast, the implementation levels of *government agencies delegating controls to customs authorities* remains sporadic with extremely low and high averages across the subregions. Central Asia and the South-Eastern Europe subregions, in particular, have significant scope for advancement in this measure. The single-country groups of the Russian Federation and the North America are evidently leading the institutional arrangement and cooperation category with 100% implementation of two measures.

Figure 12: Implementation of "institutional arrangement and cooperation" measures, 2019

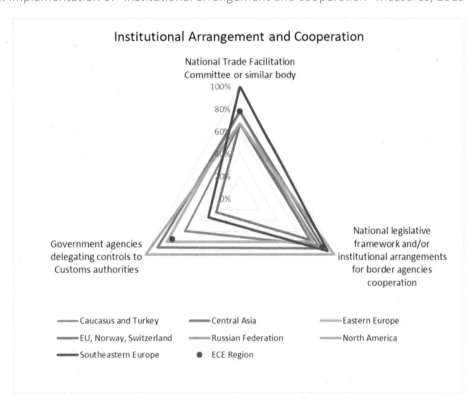

Source: United Nations Global Survey on Digital and Sustainable Trade Facilitation, 2019.

Based on the ranking of measures according to number of countries implementing them, this category remains a work-in-progress. Figure 13 shows that 64.2% of countries (27 countries) fully implemented the *national legislative framework for border agencies cooperation*. The number for the *national trade facilitation committees* is slightly lower at 61.9% (26 countries). Establishing such a committee is a requirement of the WTO Trade Facilitation Agreement. This committee acts as the focal point for coordination of the implementation of all trade facilitation measures in a country. The least implemented measure in this category was *government agencies delegating controls to customs* as only 52.3% of countries (22 countries) implemented this measure. These figures reflect the fact that implementation of institutional base or a foundation for long-term implementation of trade facilitation reforms is still an on-going process. Possibly, the definitive form of inter-agency collaboration is the delegation of authority by one or more agencies to another, as suggested by the measure *government agencies delegating controls to customs authorities*. Although the implementation of these measures is satisfactory in general, it is critical to look at the functioning of the coordination of agencies and operations of the national trade facilitation committees on the ground.

The most fully implemented measure of the three measures considered in this group is the *establishment of National Trade Facilitation Committee or similar body*. The establishment of such a committee is mandatory for all countries intent on ratifying the WTO TFA. Nearly 90% of the countries have formally established a committee or have a de facto committee in place—although not always created by a legal instrument—at least on a partial basis. However, it often remains unclear whether such a body is fully operational or has the authority and membership necessary to support effective trade facilitation reforms.

Figure 13: Implementation of "institutional arrangement and cooperation" measures, 2019

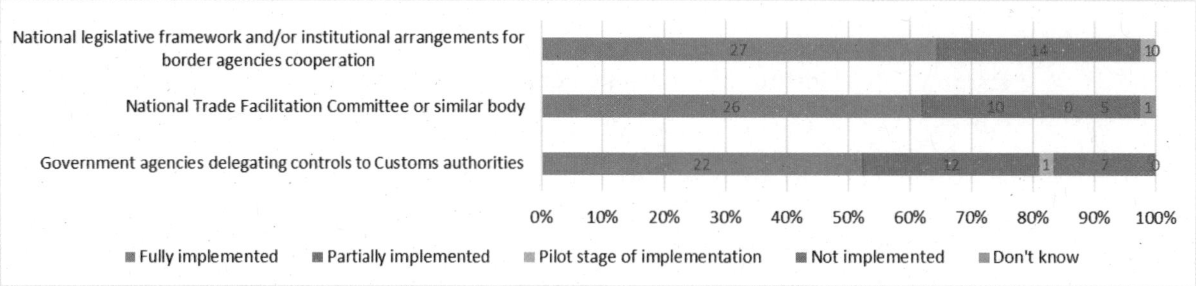

Source: United Nations Global Survey on Digital and Sustainable Trade Facilitation, 2019.

3.4 "Paperless Trade" measures

The implementation of the set of digital measures in the 'Paperless trade' category is mixed with an average implementation of 71.8% in the UNECE region. This category primarily assesses the national systems or solutions that contribute to paperless trade. The regional and subregional average levels of implementation for the nine "paperless trade" measures vary widely, as shown in Figure 14. At the regional level, the measure *automated custom system* is among the most implemented measures of all paperless trade measures included in our database. Among all the measures, the fundamentally-basic measures of *automated customs system, electronic submission of customs declaration,* and *international connection available to customs and other agencies* are the most-implemented by the subregions. The implementation of e-payment options for customs duties, fees and refunds has been proving difficult for some subregions, including Eastern and South-Eastern Europe. The *electronic single window*, a popular digital gateway for single submission of regulatory and commercial documents, has been implemented moderately, or not at all in South-Eastern Europe. The least implemented measures are *electronic application and issuance of preferential certificate of origin* and *electronic submission of air cargo manifests*.

Figure 14: Implementation of "paperless trade" measures: UNECE average, 2019

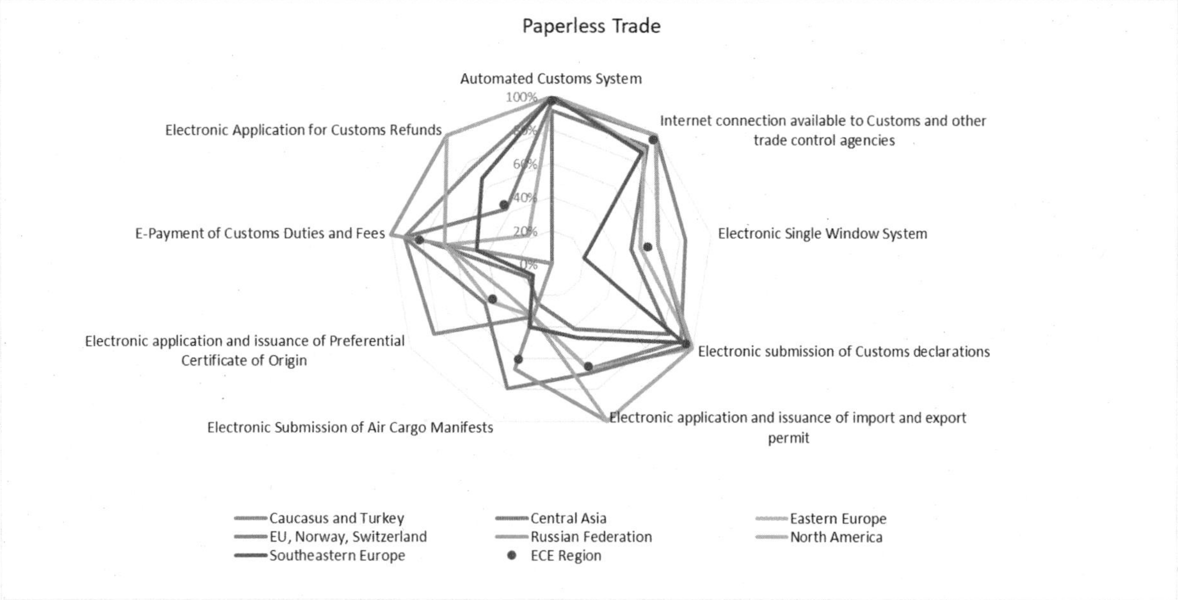

Source: United Nations Global Survey on Digital and Sustainable Trade Facilitation, 2019.

Recognizing the importance of having the basic information and communications technology infrastructure and services to enable "paperless trade", all countries of the UNECE region (100%) have fully and partially made available the measure *electronic/automated customs system*, as seen in figure 15. One hundred per cent of the countries surveyed have also fully or partially implemented the measures *Internet connection to trade control agencies at border-crossing* and *electronic submission of customs declaration*. As the UNECE region is home to many digitally-advanced countries, more than 70% of the countries surveyed either fully or partially implemented 5 out of 8 measures in this category. *Automated customs systems, internet connection available to customs and other trade agencies* and *electronic submission of customs declaration* have been implemented by all the countries surveyed. However, progress still need to be made in *electronic application for custom refunds* and *electronic application and issuance of preferential certificate of origin* as less than 50% of countries modernized their procedure.

Figure 15: Implementation of "paperless trade" measures in UNECE economies, 2019

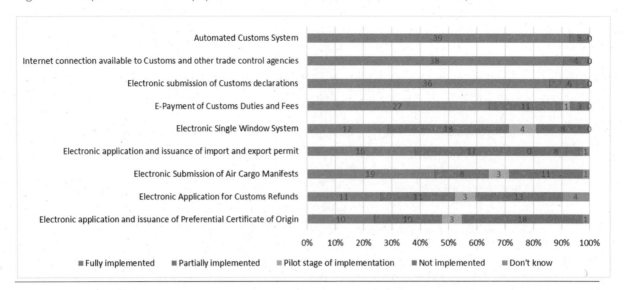

Source: United Nations Global Survey on Digital and Sustainable Trade Facilitation, 2019.3

Some relatively simple measures, such as *electronic application and issuance of import and export permit, electronic submission of air cargo manifest, electronic application and issuance of preferential Certificate of Origin, and electronic application for customs refunds* are even less implemented than single window. This could be partially explained by the fact that single window systems in most countries are developed and led by Customs and information and documents issued by other trade-related agencies are not fully automated or connected with single window.

3.5 "Cross-border paperless trade" measures

Among the six "cross-border paperless trade" measures, as shown in Figure 16, two measures, *law and regulations for electronic transactions*, and *recognized certification authority*, are basic building-blocks towards enabling the exchange and legal recognition of trade-related data and documents—not only among stakeholders within a country, but ultimately also between stakeholders along the entire international supply chain. The other four measures relate to the actual exchange of specific trade-related data and documents across borders to achieve a fully integrated paperless transformation.

Figure 16 shows the average scores for implementing the "cross-border paperless trade" measures. At the regional level, the implementation of these measures is relatively incomplete. The average implementation of the cross-border paperless trade measures in the UNECE region is 45.8%. The measures in this category attempt to assess the key policy actions for enabling exchange of trade transaction data between stakeholders internationally. It consists of a few ambitious measures, some of which have been implemented at very low levels by some UNECE economies. Some economies did not implement many of the measures. North America, represented by one country in the subregion, took bold steps by implementing four of the measures in full. *Recognized certification authority* and *laws and regulations for electronic transactions* have been attempted and achieved to a certain extent by almost all the subregions. *Electronic exchange of SPS* and *certificate of origin* have been proving to be the most challenging measures as none of the subregions achieved more than 42% implementation (except North America for one of the measures, reaching 100% implementation). In general, the low level of implementation in this category highlights that UNECE countries need to step-up with further actions beyond the legal basis or institutional readiness, nationally facilitating cross-border paperless trade.

Figure 16: Implementation of "cross-border paperless trade": measures: UNECE average, 2019

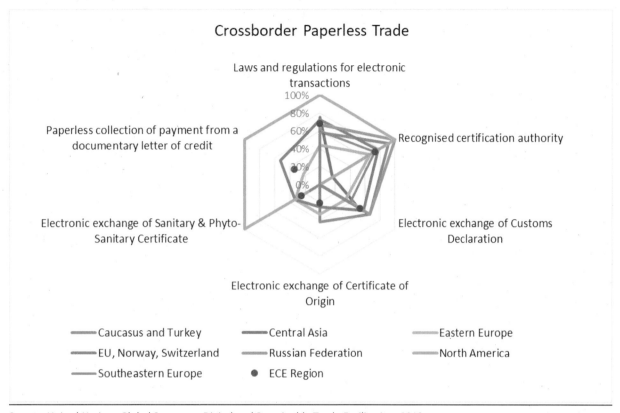

Source: United Nations Global Survey on Digital and Sustainable Trade Facilitation, 2019

Figure 17 shows the number of countries implementing the measures in this category in descending order. Many of the UNECE member states are advanced economies. Naturally, the expectation is that legal frameworks and institutions are implemented. More than 80.9% of the countries (34 countries) fully or partially implemented *laws and regulations for electronic transactions* and *recognized certification authorities*. In contrast, the measures on actual electronic exchange of SPS certificates or *Certificate of Origin* have been implemented by only 33.3% (14 countries) and 10.8% of countries (10 countries), respectively. Furthermore, more than 50% of the countries (22 or 23 countries) did not implement these measures at all.

Figure 17: Implementation of "cross-border paperless trade" measures, 2019

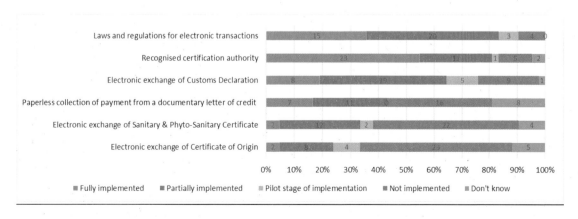

Source: United Nations Global Survey on Digital and Sustainable Trade Facilitation, 2019.

3.6 "Transit facilitation" measures

Four trade facilitation measures included in the survey relate specifically to transit facilitation and TFA Article 11 on Freedom of Transit. These measures aim to facilitate seamless and efficient border crossing of goods between a country and its neighbouring country, or a third country. These measures are particularly useful for landlocked developing countries. The UNECE membership includes several landlocked developing countries in Central Asia and Eastern Europe, and therefore this category of measures is an important performance indicator of transit facilitation. The average implementation level of "transit" measures in the region is over 83.7% across all measures. The top measure in the UNECE region includes the measure of *cooperation between agencies of countries involved in transit*.

The *cooperation between agencies of countries involved in transit* and *limiting physical examination of transit goods* are relatively well implemented by most of the subregions. As expected, the EU, Norway and Switzerland and North America have fully implemented *pre-arrival processing*, while South-Eastern Europe has the lowest average implementation for this measure. The *transit facilitation agreement* measure does not apply within the EU countries. However, it applies when it comes to non-EU European countries.

Figure 18: Implementation of "transit facilitation" measures: UNECE average, 2019

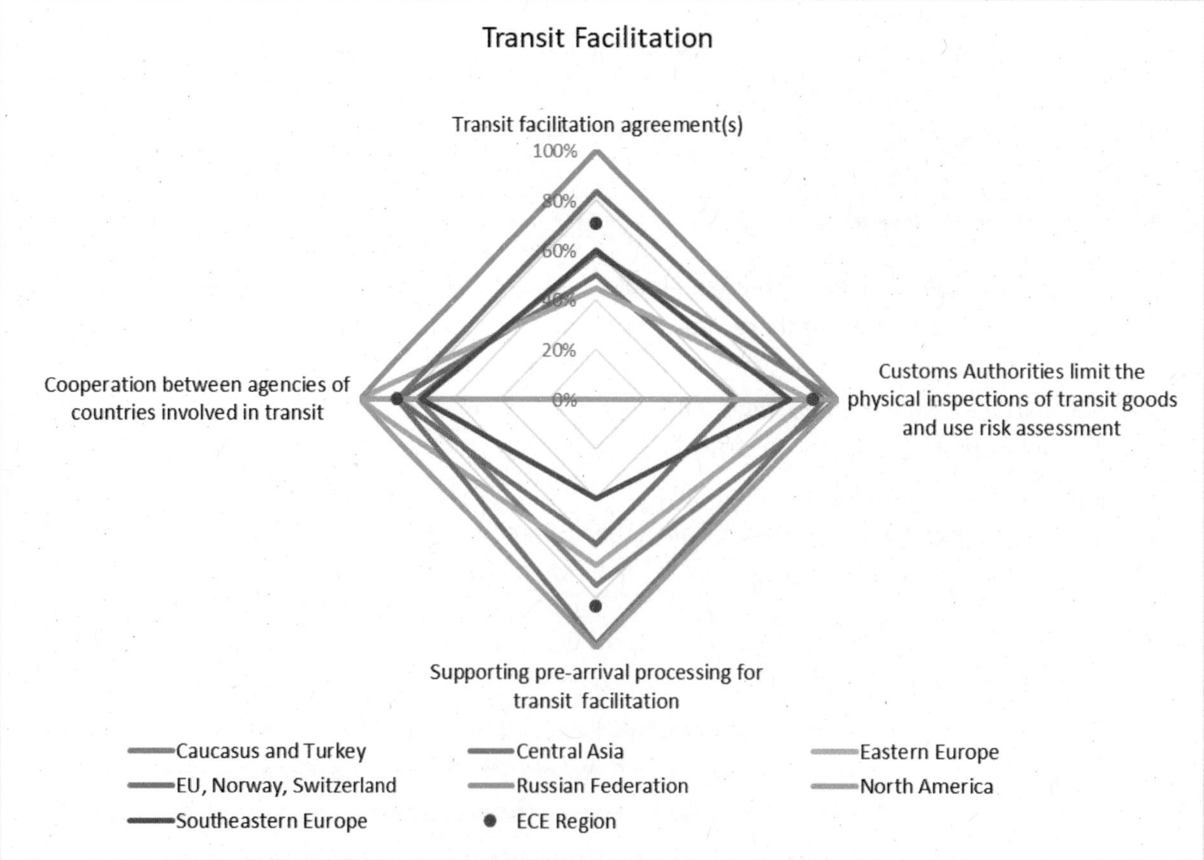

Source: United Nations Global Survey on Digital and Sustainable Trade Facilitation, 2019

The number of countries implementing "transit facilitation measures" is relatively high. In terms of implementation per measure (Figure 19), *customs authorities limiting the physical inspections of transit goods and use risk assessment* has been fully or partially implemented by 92.8% of surveyed countries (39 countries). This is followed by *cooperation between agencies of countries involved in transit* and *supporting pre-arrival processing* with 85.7% of countries (36 countries) implementing them in full or on a partial-basis. Transit facilitation agreements have been implemented by 73.8% of countries (31 countries), while 16.6% of countries (7 countries) did not implement them yet.

Figure 19: Implementation of "transit facilitation" measures, 2019

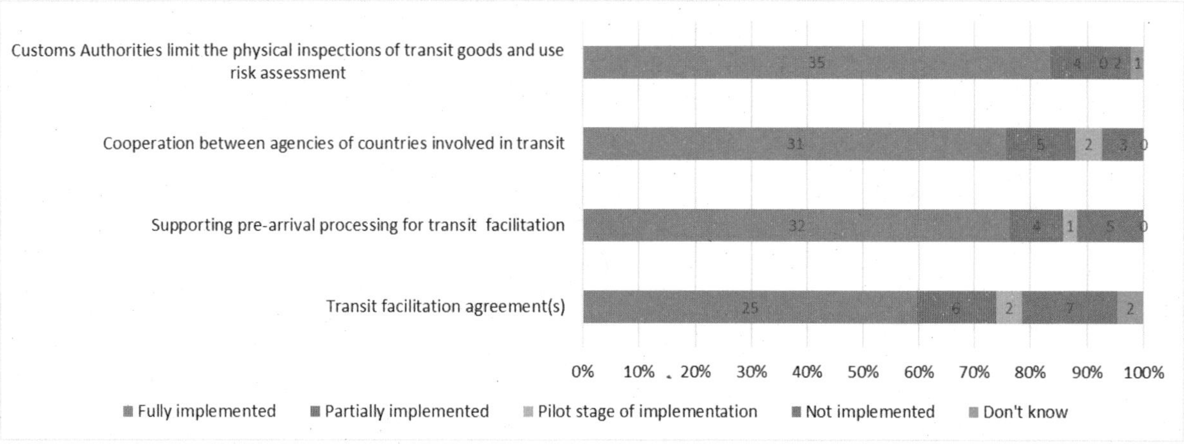

3.7 "Trade facilitation for SMEs" measures

"Trade facilitation for SMEs" measures attempt to assess the various facilities and services that allow Small and Medium-sized Enterprises (SMEs) to participate in international trade effectively and efficiently. The average implementation of the measures in this category is 43.1%, which is relatively lower than those of the general trade facilitation measures of transparency, formalities or institutional arrangement and cooperation. Some subregions, including the Russian Federation, North America and South-Eastern Europe are undertaking specific measures targeting SMEs, along with a few other subregions who are beginning to work on advancing these specific measures. *SMEs in Authorized Economic Operator (AEO) scheme*s is a relatively new provision, for which the Caucasus and Turkey subregion leads the way. In all these measures, the EU, Norway and Switzerland group seems to have lowest level of implementation. This can be explained by the fact that trade facilitation services offered in most of these countries are already easily accessible and aptly facilitate participation in international trade. Hence, separate policies for SMEs are not required.

Figure 20: Implementation of "trade facilitation for SMEs" measures: Asia-Pacific average, 2019

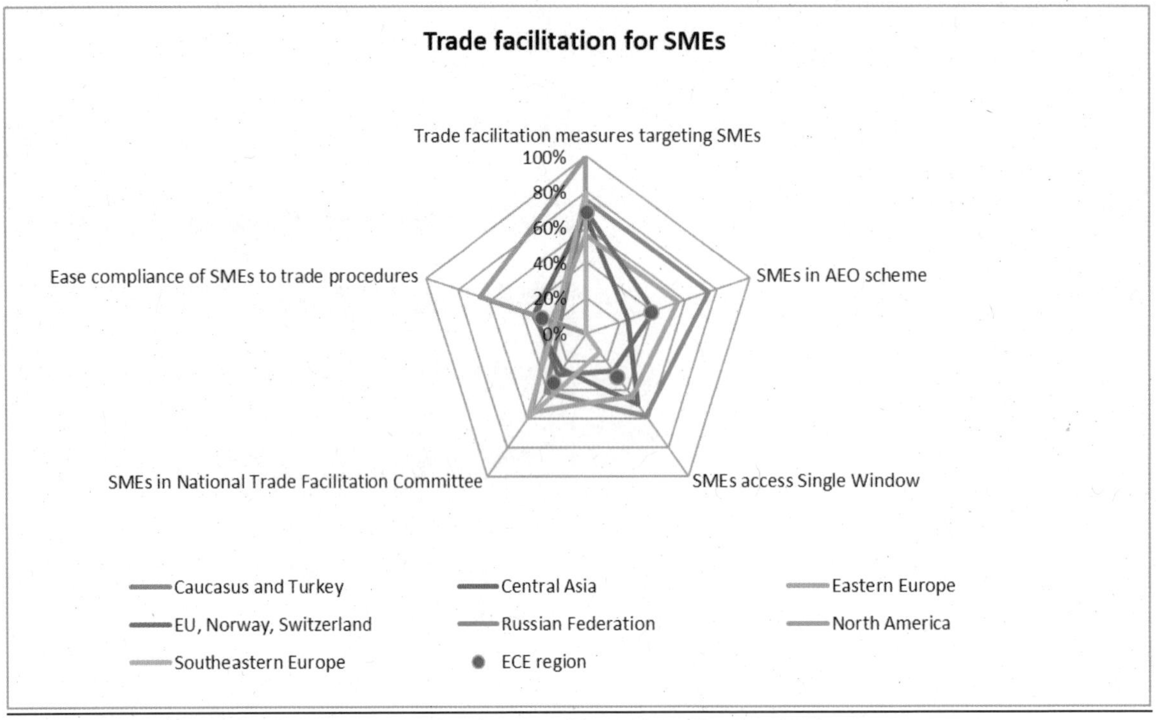

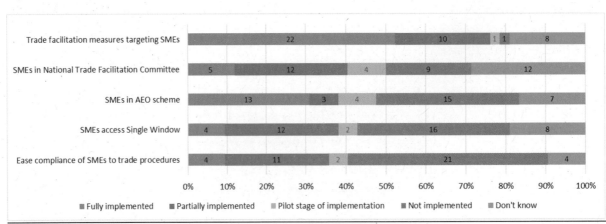

Trade facilitation for SMEs

Source: United Nations Global Survey on Digital and Sustainable Trade Facilitation, 2019.

Figure 21 shows that 76.1% of the countries (32 countries) implemented *trade facilitation measures targeting SMEs*. More than 40% of the surveyed countries (17 countries) have included representatives of *SMEs in National Trade Facilitation Committees*.

Other measures, such as facilitating *SMEs participation in the AEO scheme*, have been, at least partially, implemented by 38.09% of countries (16 countries). Provisions for *SMEs access to Single Windows* have been put in place by the same number of countries, although only four countries have implemented them in full. The measure referring to the *ease of compliance to trade procedure for SMEs*, has been implemented by 35.7% of countries (15 countries) at least partially, but half of the countries did not implement it at all.

Figure 21: Implementation of "trade facilitation for SMEs" measures, 2019

Source: United Nations Global Survey on Digital and Sustainable Trade Facilitation, 2019.

3.8 "Agricultural Trade Facilitation" Measures

The average implementation rate of "agricultural trade facilitation" measures in the UNECE region is 47.3%. Furthermore, the implementation levels (see Figure 22) vary significantly across subregions. One of the basic requirements for international trade in agriculture is to *make testing and laboratory facilities available to traders*, which was one of the most implemented measures in the UNECE region, led by the Russian Federation, and followed by Caucasus and Turkey. *Special treatment due to perishability* is moderately ensured across the subregions, while most of them are well on their way to developing *national standards and accreditation bodies*. The least-implemented measure in this category is the *electronic application and issuance of SPS certificates*. This is not surprising given the advanced nature of the measure which requires well developed electronic services.

Figure 22: Implementation of "agricultural trade facilitation" measures: UNECE average, 2019

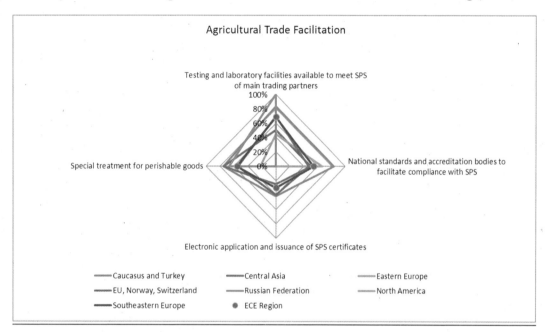

Source: United Nations Global Survey on Digital and Sustainable Trade Facilitation, 2019.

The first three measures in figure 23 are fundamental provisions for international trade in agriculture. The countries are generally mid-way through implementing these measures. In line with the analysis above, figure 23 shows that *testing and laboratory facilities for SPS compliance* have been implemented either fully or partially by 73.8% of countries (31 countries), and *special treatment for perishable goods* at least partially, in 64.2% of countries (27 countries). Likewise, *national standards and accreditation bodies* have been made available, at least partially, in the same number of countries. *Electronic application and issuance of SPS certificates* is particularly challenging in the region. Full implementation of this measure is lower than 10%. *Electronic application and issuance of SPS certificates* has been implemented, at least partially, by only 38.09% of countries (16 countries). This may be explained by the fact that current common practice on the import side is still to accept paper certificates, and also by a low level of adoption of digital solutions by agencies other than customs.

Figure 23: Implementation of "Agricultural Trade Facilitation" measures, 2019

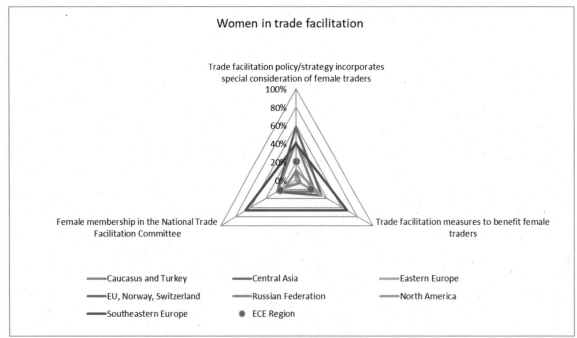

Source: United Nations Global Survey on Digital and Sustainable Trade Facilitation, 2019.

3.9 "Women in trade facilitation" measures

The regional and subregional average levels of implementation for the three "women in trade facilitation" measures, as shown in figure 24, appear very low. The regional average implementation rate for this category is only 20.4%, and ranges from 19% for the measure of *trade facilitation measures to benefit female traders* to 21.43% for the measure *female membership in the National Trade Facilitation Committees*. It is worth noting that in the developed economies group of countries (i.e. the EU, Norway and Switzerland) the provisions are suitable for women traders, as women traders do not necessarily need targeted facilitation approaches. Implementation of these measures are moderate in the subregions of South-Eastern Europe and Central Asia, while other subregions (non-developed economies) significantly lag behind in this category of measures.

Figure 24: Implementation of "women in trade facilitation" measures: UNECE average, 2019

Source: United Nations Global Survey on Digital and Sustainable Trade Facilitation, 2019.

More specifically, as shown in Figures 25, none of the three measures have been fully implemented by more than 9.5% of countries (4 countries). In about one third (30.9% or 13 countries) of the countries surveyed, *female membership in National Trade Facilitation Committees* has been fully or partially implemented, while in almost half of the countries (47.6% or 20 countries) it was not entirely clear whether female membership in these Committees had not been ensured, or if it was not considered an issue since there were already female members existing. The relative lack of awareness on this topic was reflected in the high level of responses that stated "don't know" in the survey.

Figure 25: Implementation of "women in trade facilitation" measures, 2019

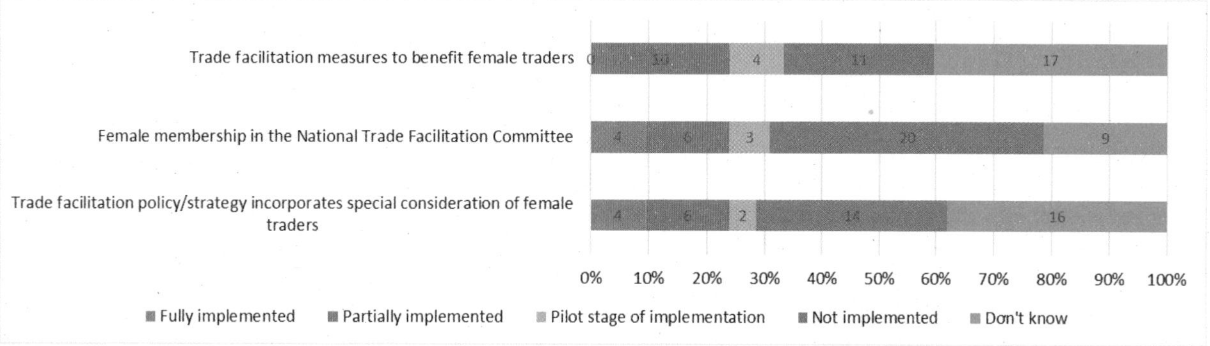

Source: United Nations Global Survey on Digital and Sustainable Trade Facilitation, 2019

3.10 "Trade finance for trade facilitation" measures

Trade finance has been a key catalyst of the expansion of international trade in the past century. Given the increasing importance of trade finance in the international trading system, "trade finance" has been incorporated as a new group of measures into the 2019 Survey. The intention was to gauge the rate of implementation of digital provisions for these measures and also the range of financial services in the UNECE region. However, despite their importance, the "trade finance for trade facilitation" group of measures have the lowest implementation rates in the Survey. Indeed, the UNECE regional average of implementation is only 18.3%. This is mainly due to the absence of integration of trade finance services into mainstream digital solutions, as reflected in the limited access that single window systems provide to traders.

Figure 26: Implementation of "trade finance for trade facilitation" measures: UNECE average, 2019

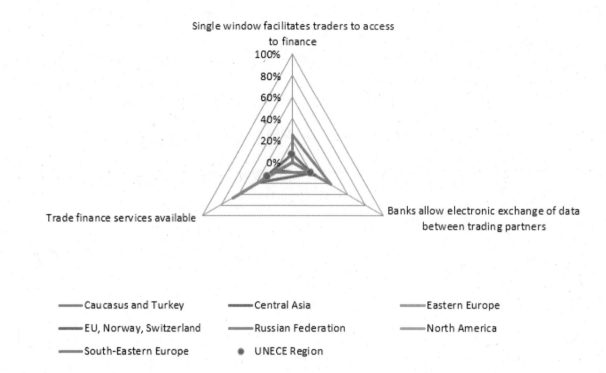

Source: United Nations Global Survey on Digital and Sustainable Trade Facilitation, 2019.

In terms of number of countries, more than half of the countries either did not implement or did not have definitive answers on the implementation of these measures. The most implemented measure of all three was the measure on *trade finance services being available*. However, it only reaches 30.9% for full or partial implementation. Only 19% of the countries appear to have banks that allow electronic exchange of data between trading partners (or banks in other countries) to reduce dependence on paper documentation and advance digital trade.

The above is not unexpected as these measures are special in nature. For example, while establishing single windows is a standard type of measure, facilitating access to finance through a single window is a much-more advanced measure for a country. These results suggest that there is a need for trade finance services to be further developed in many countries of the region. The high rates of "Don't know" also point to the fact that the trade facilitation experts and officials who provided or validated the survey did not have detailed information about these measures.

Figure 27: Implementation of "trade finance for trade facilitation" measures in UNECE economies, 2019

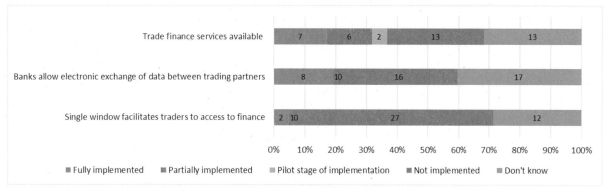

Source: United Nations Global Survey on Digital and Sustainable Trade Facilitation, 2019.

3.11   Progress and challenges in implementation

Figure 28 shows the 10 trade facilitation measures which have been most fully-implemented in the region by 2019. It shows that across the UNECE region, countries have focused their efforts on improving measures like automated customs systems, internet connection availability for customs and other trade control agencies, and electronic submission of customs declarations. In these areas many have achieved full implementation over the past years. Many countries have also worked on post-clearance audits and customs authorities limiting the physical inspections of the goods. None of the top measures on the list are from the inclusive categories (i.e. agricultural trade facilitation, trade facilitation for SMEs, women in trade facilitation or trade finance for trade facilitation).

Figure 28: Most fully-implemented trade facilitation measures in UNECE (42 countries)

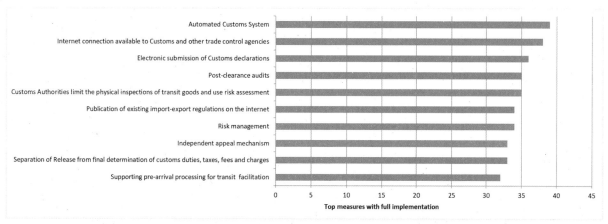

Source: United Nations Global Survey on Digital and Sustainable Trade Facilitation, 2019

Box 2: Sustainable trade facilitation in the transition economies

Journey towards sustainable trade facilitation in the transition economies

The performance of sustainable trade facilitation measures is assessed through three categories: trade facilitation for SMEs, trade facilitation and agricultural trade, and women in trade facilitation. Implementation of these measures supports the achievement of specific targets of the 2030 Sustainable Development Agenda, specifically for gender equality, SMEs, and address special sectoral needs in agriculture. The figure below shows the average implementation of the transition economies in four subregions. Caucasus and Turkey lead the way in trade facilitation for SMEs, passing the half-way mark. This particular subregion is also the highest performer with an average implementation above 70% in the trade facilitation and agriculture trade area. Central Asia also made great strides in this area, reaching 50% implementation. In the women in trade facilitation category, South-Eastern Europe achieved the highest implementation with slightly less than 58% implementation. All these subregions need to strengthen their efforts in these areas, which would ultimately speed their progress toward sustainable development.

Overview of sustainable trade facilitation in the UNECE subregions

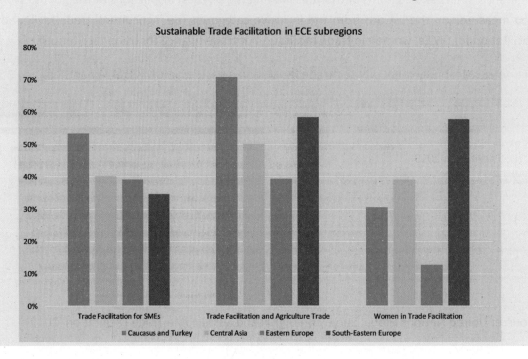

4. Conclusion and way forward

The purpose of trade facilitation is primarily to increase the efficiency, and reduce the costs of trading across borders. This not only leads to higher economic gains, but also contributes to more inclusive economic gains, especially for women, SMEs, and for key development sectors like agriculture. Figure 29 shows a strong negative correlation between trade facilitation implementation and trade costs in the UNECE region. In fact, trade costs (excluding tariff, tariff equivalent) tend to be lower for countries with high trade facilitation implementation.

Figure 29: Trade facilitation implementation and trade costs (tariff equivalent)

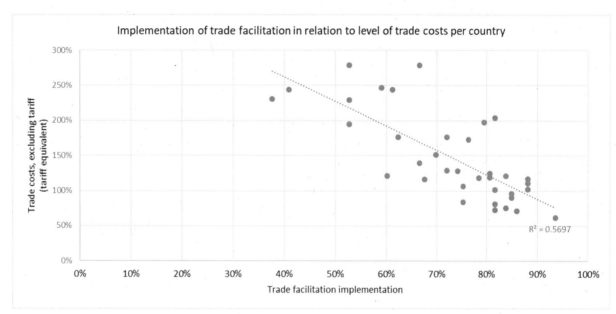

Source: ESCAP-World Bank Trade Cost Database and the United Nations Global Survey on Digital and Sustainable Trade Facilitation 2019

The UNECE region's average implementation has increased to 72.6% since the last Survey in 2017. The average implementation is greater than the global average of 62.7%. Among the surveyed countries, there are 25 developed economies, 16 economies in transition and 1 developing economy. In general, developed economies tend to reach higher trade facilitation implementation. However, some of the transition economies have caught up, reaching high levels of performance.

In terms of measures, most general trade facilitation measures are implemented in full. For example, transparency and formalities categories have reached more than 80% implementation on average, whereas paperless trade has reached 71.8%. But the biggest gap remains between the paperless trade and the cross-border paperless trade categories, with the latter reaching 45.8% implementation only.

Implementation for the sustainable trade facilitation measure is at the lower end of the spectrum. Measures for the agriculture sector have been implemented at 47.3% only, on average, and there is much room for improvement in the implementation of measures for the SMEs, which has reached 43.1%. The facilitation of trade for women and that trade finance categories remain at the bottom, with implementation rates hovering around 20%. This shows that the trade facilitation agenda needs to address inclusive measures to ensure a greater development impact in trade and a more robust contribution to the achievement of the Sustainable Development Goals of the United Nations 2030 Agenda.

Figure 30: Moving up the ladder in trade facilitation implementation

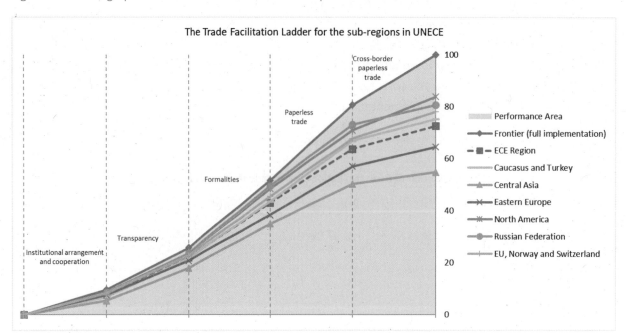

The trade facilitation ladder, as shown in Figure 30, reviews the performance of the step-by-step measures, considering the cumulative scores (converted to percentage) of the five categories. While developed economies are close to full implementation at each step of the ladder, for non-developed economies the gap between their level and full implementation remains large—especially for the paperless trade and cross-border paperless trade categories.

Trade facilitation reform is a continuous process. To obtain the maximum benefit from such reforms, a step-by-step approach should be followed. According to the UN/CEFACT Policy Recommendations and Guidelines, solid institutional frameworks and multi-stakeholder cooperation and consultation mechanisms need to be in place as an important enabling factor of effective reform efforts. This should be followed by efforts to ensure full access to trade-related information to increase the transparency of processes. The next step is to address formalities, which should ideally simplify and streamline processes. Further legal frameworks, systems and approaches for implementation of digital measures should be put in place. Finally, the measures for cross-border paperless trade transactions should be implemented. Therefore, a systematic approach should be followed.